Of bloom ethereal the light footed dews.

9. Wind pretty fresh
from No. Wt. all day
— weather cleared
Mercury at 82. —

10. Clear with the Wind
Southerly — Mer y at 84

11. Wind all No. Wt. all day
a little rain having fel
len in the Night but
not on my Farms M. 81

12. Little or no wind — Mer
cury at 83.

13. Calm and clear all
day — Mer y. at 85

14. Very little wind and
clear — Mer y 91.

15. Last Night extreme
ly warm — clear &
calm — Mer 88

16. Very warm with the
Wind at No. Mer 90
— fine Rain in the af
ter noon — suff.t to wet the E

17. Appearances of Rain
most part of the day
but none fell — feed
yard — Went up to the
Fed.l City

18. Warm with appear
ances of Rain in the
afternoon — but none
fell. In the City all day

19. Went by the bridge
at the little falls home
G.e Tally & returned home
in the afternoon

20. Clear & warm Mer
cury at 83.

21. Much such a day as
yesterday — M. 83.

22. Warm morning & cloudy
with very fine showers
from 11 oClock in the Mor
ng until near 3 oClock
watering the gr. thoroughly
Mer y 80.

WASHINGTON'S MOUNT VERNON

Washington's Mount Vernon

WASHINGTON'S MOUNT VERNON

Photographs by Taylor Lewis, Jr.
Text by Joanne Young

Holt, Rinehart and Winston
New York, Chicago, San Francisco

Photographs: Copyright © 1973
by Taylor Biggs Lewis, Jr.
Text: Copyright © 1973 by Joanne B. Young
All rights reserved,
including the right to reproduce this book
or portions thereof in any form.
Published simultaneously in Canada by
Holt, Rinehart and Winston of Canada, Limited.
ISBN: 0–03–003961–4
Library of Congress Catalog Card Number: 72–91565
First Edition
Designer: Robert Reed
Printed in the United States of America

The drawing of the
Mount Vernon Kitchen Garden
is reprinted with permission
from Mount Vernon: An Illustrated Handbook
© 1972 by Mount Vernon Ladies' Association.

The endpapers are reproduced
from George Washington's diary (1797)
and are reprinted with permission
of Mount Vernon Ladies' Association.

In all U.S. history, there are few heroes so well known as George Washington—Father of His Country, first President, Commander-in-Chief of the Continental Army—and few men whose personalities have remained so elusive. To understand the man instead of the legend, we decided to take a long look at his land and his home, where he was most himself and where he indelibly printed his own design on the architecture, the gardens, and the landscape.

Perhaps in this way we could see him, as Joshua Brooks did in 1799, riding in from his daily inspection of his farms: "About half past two the General returned. He was dressed in a blue great coat, large buttons; blue overalls and bespattered boots. . . ."

In doing so, we came to know Mount Vernon in every season, at every time of day from dawn to moonrise, and in every kind of weather—hot sun, spring rain, snow, and fog. As we walked his roads and fields and riverside, shared his view from Mount Vernon windows, enjoyed the shade of the trees he planted, we began to feel a rapport with the man who preferred to be known as "Farmer Washington." This feeling grew as we read his daily diary entries, and the letters he wrote to friends, family, and especially the Mount Vernon managers.

His subtle sense of humor flashed, as in the letter he drafted for Martha to copy to Mrs. Samuel (Eliza) Powel of Philadelphia on July 14, 1797: "Upon slight foundation it sometimes happens that large superstructures are erected. . . . The report respecting the General's having a serious attack of the ague and fever is equally groundless. On a hot day in May, he threw off his flannels; and a sudden change of the weather at night gave him a cold, which disordered but never confined him. This is all the foundation of *that* report."

His love for Martha's small children, Patsy and Jack, and later for her grandchildren, Nelly and Washie, whom they informally adopted after Jack's death at Yorktown, was as strong as any father's. It shines through his warm letter of advice to the teen-age Nelly, about to attend her first ball in Georgetown, who had declared "a perfect apathy for the youth of the present day." "Men and women," he wrote back to her, "feel the same inclination toward each other *now* that they always have done, and which they will continue to do, until there is a new order of things; and you, as others have done, may find that the passions of your sex are easier raised than allayed. Do not, therefore, boast too soon, nor too strongly of your insensibility."

In 1781, upon hearing that a British man-of-war had anchored off Mount Vernon and Lund Washington, his manager, had complied with its officers' demand for refreshments, the General's infrequent anger flared. ". . .That which gives me most concern is, that you should go on board the enemy's vessels, and furnish them with refreshments. It would have been a less painful circumstance to me to have heard, that in consequence of your non-compliance with their request, they had burnt my House and laid the Plantation in ruins."

But it is not only George Washington who becomes three-dimensional at Mount Vernon—the pretty little widow whom he married, Martha Custis, comes into focus also. She wonders if the housework is being done in her absence. ("Make Nathan clean his kitchen and every thing in it and about it very well.") Her affection shines through as she writes to Mrs. Powel: "My pretty boy [Washie] is so pleased with the book you sent him that he has read it over and over. . . ." She seems especially human as she overcomes her fear of being vaccinated for smallpox when she faces an alternative far worse to her: not to be able to stay with her husband in the winter camps where smallpox is prevalent.

It is sad for historians that Martha Washington's instinctive sense of privacy, set aside so often for the demands of public life, asserted itself in the end. Shortly before she died, she burned the treasured packet of letters which Washington had written to her over the years. Two remain, and they speak volumes—one written from Philadelphia in 1775 when he accepted command of the Colonial Army says: "I shall feel no pain from the toil or danger of the campaign; my unhappiness will flow from the uneasiness I know you will feel from being left alone. . . . I should enjoy more real happiness in a month with you at home than I have the most distant prospect of finding abroad, if my stay were to be seven times seven years."

Essentially, then, *Washington's Mount Vernon* is a love story—of a man for his family, and theirs for him, and of a man for his home and his gardens and his land.

Where quotations are not identified, they are from George Washington's diaries, with no attempt at editing the eighteenth-century spelling, punctuation, or capitalization. Except where otherwise noted, all letters are from him, and most appear in the Library of Congress's collection *The Writings of George Washington*. Our sincere thanks go to the Mount Vernon staff and the Mount Vernon Ladies' Association for their superb cooperation and permission to quote from letters in their collection—many previously unpublished.

Joanne Young
Taylor Lewis

The buds of every kind of tree and shrub are swelling—the tender leaves of many had unfolded—the apricot blossoms were putting forth—the peaches and cherries were upon the point of doing the same. The leaves of the apple trees were coming out, those of the weeping willow and the lilac had been out many days and were the first to show themselves. . . . The red bud had begun to open . . . the dogwood had swelled into buttons.

The April wind is cold off the Potomac, a throwback to winter. It blows the lilacs in the North Grove, and they toss their purple heads in lively affirmation of the day, the season, and the general air of new life from old roots.

How old, indeed, are the roots of Mount Vernon—older than the nation itself, or the home of its first President. They go back to 1674 when George Washington's great-grandfather, John Washington, patented the homesite, calling it Hunting Creek Plantation; and were half a century old when his father, Augustine, acquired the property. April buds bloomed and faded sixty-one times on the Washington land before three-year-old George moved there with his family to the modest house his father built. Like the blowing lilacs, the house branched out from this central core.

The flower garden, warm within its protective boxwood hedge, looks freshly washed, every tulip and daffodil turning a shining face to the sun like children in church on Easter Sunday. The wind roars through the rose garden, propelling a mockingbird so fast on its flight above the gravel path that it almost collides head-on with a strolling visitor.

Looking as gnarled and sturdy as the trunks of the crape myrtle trees, a gardener is working the ground gently around the pansies and candy tuft with his hoe. He seems a worthy successor to John Christian Ehler, Philip Bader, and the others who cultivated these gardens in Washington's time.

To Robert Cary & Co., London
November 22, 1791

I have requested him to get me a Gardner. . . . I do not desire any of your fine fellows who will content themselves with planning of Work, I want a Man that will labour hard, knowing at the same time how to keep a Garden in good Order and sow seeds in their proper Season in ground that he has prepared well for the reception of them.

Washington's care in choosing a gardener was based on personal knowledge of the job's demands, and a strong sense that the growing of crops as well as trees and garden plants, required more than a green thumb.

To Mrs. Eliza Powel, December 18, 1797: "When all things will be blooming here in the spring except the withering proprietors of this mansion, [we hope] that you will carry into effect the long promised visit to this retreat."

In his Botanical Garden, behind the Salt House and the Spinning House, he constantly conducted well-documented experiments to find out which variety of seeds grew best in Mount Vernon soil, and which combination of fertilizer and soil of various types would produce the best yield. Before the word had meaning outside of a dictionary, he was an ecologist, a believer in scientific agriculture, who studied the many moods of nature daily because he found her an enigmatic mistress, well worth the wooing. Ten years before the American Revolution, he devised a plan of crop rotation to increase the fertility of his fields.

Although the Master of Mount Vernon had strict requirements for his gardener, he did his best to make the job attractive. In his contract of April 23, 1787, with Philip Bader, Washington spells out in good humor the special benefits offered:

In consideration that he will . . . industriously perform . . . every part of his duty as a Gardner . . . and that he will not . . . suffer himself to be disguised with liquor except on the times hereafter mentioned, he is allowed four dollars at Christmas, with which he may be drunk four days and nights; two dollars at Easter to effect the same purpose; two dollars at Whitsuntide to be drunk for two days; a dram in the morning and a drink of grog at dinner at noon.

Along a footworn path beside the split rail fence bordering a pasture where cows are grazing, the red bud trees show their delicate blossoms. Violets hide shyly in the grass which is polka-dotted with dandelions.

It is a day for spring cleaning, for throwing windows open to let the musty, dusty smell of winter out and let the scent of hyacinths come in. Martha Washington would have known what to do with such a day!

From Martha Washington
to Colonel Clement Biddle, Philadelphia
merchant

We are much in want of mops and clamps for scouring brushes. Will you get 6 of each and two closths baskets, 1 larger than the other.

In the Wash House, shirts, pants, and petticoats flap on the line; and in the Salt House, the fish nets are caught by wind also, and tap their corks impatiently against the walls.

As shadows begin to lengthen, the wind subsides; and the sun's warmth becomes more apparent. A lazy spotted dog sleeps in the middle of a lane, his old bones drinking in the sun, tired from a morning of following the red tractor which has been plowing a field for spring planting.

April—that delicious, capricious month when winter is past and summer is not quite here,

Left:
Along a pasture fence

Below:
The Washhouse
To Tobias Lear: "I do not believe the House can be better supplied with washer women."

Double-flowering almond

Crown imperial

Double-flowering tulip

Primrose

whose mood is like a young girl's with warm smiles one minute and tears the next—has seen both large and small events at Mount Vernon.

April 18, 1770

Patcy Custis and Milly Posey went to Colo. Mason's to the Dancing School.

April 5, 1771

Turned the water of Doeg Run into my Mill Race, which seemed to afford Water enough for both Mills, one of which is constantly employed in Grinding up my own Wheat.

April 17, 1771

Began to Plant Corn at my Mill Plantation.

April was only four days past when the forty-three-year-old Washington rode off in his coach for Philadelphia to represent Virginia in the Second Continental Congress in 1775, and his planter's eye looked attentively at the first signs of green in his fields as he left, expecting to be gone only a few weeks. Which of the varieties of wheat he had planted this spring would do best? He would be anxious to see when he returned. But events in Philadelphia changed all that, as he wrote to his younger brother, John Augustine:

I am now to bid adieu to you, and to every kind of domestic ease for a while. I am embarked on a wide ocean, boundless in its prospect, and in which, perhaps, no safe harbor is to be found. I have been called upon by the unanimous voice of the Colonies to take the command of the Continental army.

Six long years passed before he found that harbor and returned to his beloved Mount Vernon for a brief stay on his way to Yorktown. It would take two more years before he could resign his commission at Annapolis and again take up his life as a farmer, which in his heart he had never relinquished. During the long, bitter frustrating war —and perhaps as an antidote to it—he kept a firm, if distant, hand on affairs at home, carefully reading the weekly reports from his manager, Lund Washington. He answered them in minute detail with instructions on every facet of the plantation work from proper planting of seed to caring for the poor who might need corn when harvests were meager. His homecoming was joyous; but in a sense he had never left.

Bees were swarming and apple trees in bloom on May 9, 1787, when he "crossed from Mount Vernon to Dr. Digges a little after sunrise" on his barge, and turned his horses again to Philadelphia to head Virginia's delegation to the Constitutional Congress. And it was April, two years later, when with "peculiar gratification" but great personal reservations he received the official

Left:
Seal on Washington's trunk

Below:
The Washingtons' bedroom

Facing page:
Martha Washington's writing desk; above it, a portrait of her granddaughter Martha Custis Peter

news of his election as the first President of the United States. Reluctantly he "bade adieu" to Mount Vernon, to private life, and to "domestic felicity" in order "to render service to my country in obedience to its calls. . . ."

Appropriately, it was almost April once more, with her festival of bloom and new leaves uncurling, when Washington arrived at Mount Vernon in 1797 for his happiest homecoming of all. The journey from Philadelphia, after light-heartedly turning over the Presidency to John Adams, was historic, but it also included moments known to any family man.

To his secretary, Tobias Lear,
en route to Mount Vernon
March 9, 1797

On one side I am called upon to remember the Parrot, and on the other to remember the dog. For my own part I should not pine much if both were forgot.

When the carriage turned in through the Mount Vernon gates, he had a sense of satisfaction from knowing he had served his country in every capacity it had asked of him to the best of his considerable ability; but now he had other goals in mind.

To Oliver Wolcott
May 15, 1797

To make and sell a little flour, to repair houses going fast to ruin, to build one for the security of my papers of a public nature, and to amuse myself with Agricultural and rural pursuits, will constitute employment for the years I have to remain on this terrestrial Globe. If . . . I could now and then meet friends I esteem, it would fill the measure . . . but, if ever this happens, it must be under my own vine and fig-tree, as I do not think it probable that I shall go beyond twenty miles from them.

If in comparison to the past two decades, Washington felt that life at Mount Vernon was tranquil, it was by no means idle! Far from spending many hours stretched out "under his own vine and fig tree," he plunged into so many repairs and renovations which had been postponed during the years of his Presidency that he soon found himself in a plight familiar to many remodelers.

To William Heath

In a word, I am already surrounded by joiners, masons and painters, and such is my anxiety to be out of their hands that I have scarcely a room to put a friend into, or to sit in myself, without the music of hammers and the odiferous scent of paint.

But he was not the only one overjoyed to become a permanent resident at Mount Vernon again. During his two terms as President while Martha Washington sometimes felt herself "more like a State prisoner than anything else," she had been homesick,

First floor guest room

The pantry

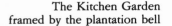

The Kitchen Garden
framed by the plantation bell

longing for her own parlor, her own pantry, and her own view of the river below the hill.

Looking back over the long years of self-imposed exile in order to be with her husband, first in various Army headquarters during the war, and then New York and Philadelphia during his Presidency, she recalled the hope of this moment that had sustained her.

*From Martha Washington
to Mrs. Mercy Otis Warren
November 26, 1789*

I had long since placed all the prospects of my future worldly happiness in the still enjoyments of the fireside at Mount Vernon.

She felt a joyous sense of freedom as she saw to the unpacking of their belongings sent by boat from Philadelphia—Nelly's harpsichord, a new parlor carpet, the large looking glasses, Washie's schoolbooks (she must make him study harder). Each box that arrived meant one thing to her—they were home at last!

From the South Lane, the plantation bell rings, signaling the end of another working day. Latches click and keys turn in the locks of doors to storehouses and other outbuildings; workmen head in from the fields and garden, tools over their shoulders. The sun slips behind the red-shingled roof of the stable, and a mockingbird murmurs in the magnolia tree.

The appearance of the Weather for sevl. days past has given the greatest room to apprehend the Rust—the mornings close, foggy and calm; the Evenings Cloudy and sometimes raining, Heavy Dews at Nights and warm Sultry days.

Summer

It is the hour before dawn. The Old Mill Road lies deserted, the leaves on overhanging trees scarcely moving on this windless morning; but it is blissfully cool. Yesterday's heat is momentarily forgotten, although the road itself still holds a faint warmth to bare feet luxuriating in shoeless freedom.

A tangle of blackberry bushes on either side of the West Gate, just ahead at the end of the road, is faintly silvered with summer dust. The gate itself, its strap hinges, and the fence posts with their cone-shaped caps, are wet with dew.

Beyond it, fog lies in the hollows and stretches a misty curtain over the mansion house that can just be seen between the gate houses, beyond the meadow and the Bowling Green. Now the sky turns faintly pink behind the house, and a faint blush colors the treetops above the fog. A startled crow flies out of the cedar trees and takes off with an ear-splitting cawing above the quiet meadow. A rabbit in search of breakfast hops along the Serpentine Path, bold in the safety of morning shadows.

The sun begins to rise, turning the sky to gold and sending probing fingers through the green trees. It changes the dew from silver to crystal wherever it touches, and dapples the road with shadow patterns.

August 1, 1771

Began to sow wheat in the Neck with wheat steep'd in Brine and allum.

Through this farm gate George Washington rode each morning that he was in residence here, at an hour only a little later than this one, to inspect the other four farms that made up Mount Vernon Plantation. Sometimes he turned his horse toward Union Farm, at the confluence of the Potomac and Dogue Creek. On other days, he headed for Dogue Run or Muddy Hole Farms, north of the river beyond the hundreds of acres of woodland which the plantation required. (He needed ten wooded acres, roughly, for each Mount Vernon fireplace, not only to heat the houses and quarters in cold weather, but to run the forge, heat water for the busy laundry, cure the sides of bacon and plump Virginia hams hanging in the Smokehouse, and keep cooking fires burning in the kitchen.)

When crops or livestock at the River Farm needed his attention, he took his barge across Little Hunting Creek to his land on the east. One frequent stop on his daily rounds was motivated by

Facing page:
Sundial in the courtyard, at the west entrance

Sun streams through a pasture fence.

sentiment instead of managerial duties
—at the pasture to which his chestnut
battle horse, Nelson, had been lovingly
retired after the surrender at
Yorktown. Now the old horse had
green fields in summer, a snug stable
when it was cold, and the leisure
which he had so richly earned.

To Secretary of War James McHenry
May 29, 1791

I might tell [you] that I begin my diurnal
course with the sun; that, if my hirelings are
not in their places at that time, I send them
messages of sorrow for their indisposition;
that, having put these wheels in motion, I
examine the state of things further; . . . that,
by the time I have accomplished these matters,
breakfast (a little after seven o'clock) . . .
is ready; that, this being over, I mount my
horse and ride round my farms, which
employs me until it is time to dress for
dinner. . . . The usual time of sitting at
table, a walk, and tea brings me within the
dawn of candlelight. . . .

Mount Vernon is awake now.
The mourning doves are predicting
rain, but peach-colored clouds, softly
churning in a pale blue sky, do not
look threatening. The fog has almost
disappeared except just above the
Potomac where it hovers like another
river, suspended in the quiet air.

Dew, which still covers the clapboard
front of the office at the head of the
North Lane, outlines the pattern of

the studs of the building, the slanted line of the brace. It is caught in the cobwebs that have appeared overnight in every corner of fence rail and post, and which cover the tops of the boxwood in such profusion that a gardener's helper has to sweep them off with a broom.

"Crazy spiders!" he laughs, shaking his head. It is as though the spiders had some premonition that these sweltering days of summer would soon be over and were weaving prodigious supplies of blankets to cover everything during the winter ahead.

The flock of crows in the Wilderness that borders the Serpentine Walk around the green are sending up a noisy racket, and squirrels are busy in the pecan trees, scampering about with an air of important business to be attended to.

In the flower garden—a blaze of color from the deep purple-red of crape myrtles to the gold of feathercomb, the brilliant red and yellow of snapdragons, and the pale pink of spider flowers—butterflies are having a field day. They hover in fluttering crowds above the flowers while swarms of pollen-laden bees dart in and out with an insistent humming, periodically taking off over the brick wall for their hives in the Kitchen Garden. Their honeycombs will soon be overflowing and ready for "harvest."

A crape myrtle in the Upper Garden

A beehive in the Kitchen Garden

Spiderflower

Snapdragon

Prickly lantana

Not far from the beehives, a mockingbird perches on the rim of the dipping well, next to a copper watering pot. It drinks its fill and trills a few notes before flying off for breakfast among the grapevines. The fruit on the espaliered apple trees bordering the walks is turning pink, and the mockingbird will no doubt stop there for dessert.

Fat robins stalk the newly cultivated furrows among the artichoke and asparagus, the plants silver in the sun's early slanting rays. Dusky red tops of beets are showing above the dark earth in their tidy rows, and the pole beans are thick with green pods. Martha Washington remembered how the Kitchen Garden looked on summer mornings when she wrote from Philadelphia to her niece, Fanny Bassett Washington, that they would soon be home for a visit. Beautiful young Fanny (who had married George Augustine Washington, the General's nephew, at Mount Vernon, October 15, 1785) was the mansion's little mistress and keeper of the keys to its many doors during the eight years of Washington's Presidency.

*From Martha Washington
to Fanny Bassett Washington
July 1, 1792*

Impress it on the gardner to have everything in his garden that will be necessary in the House Keeping way—as vegetables is the best part of our living in the country.

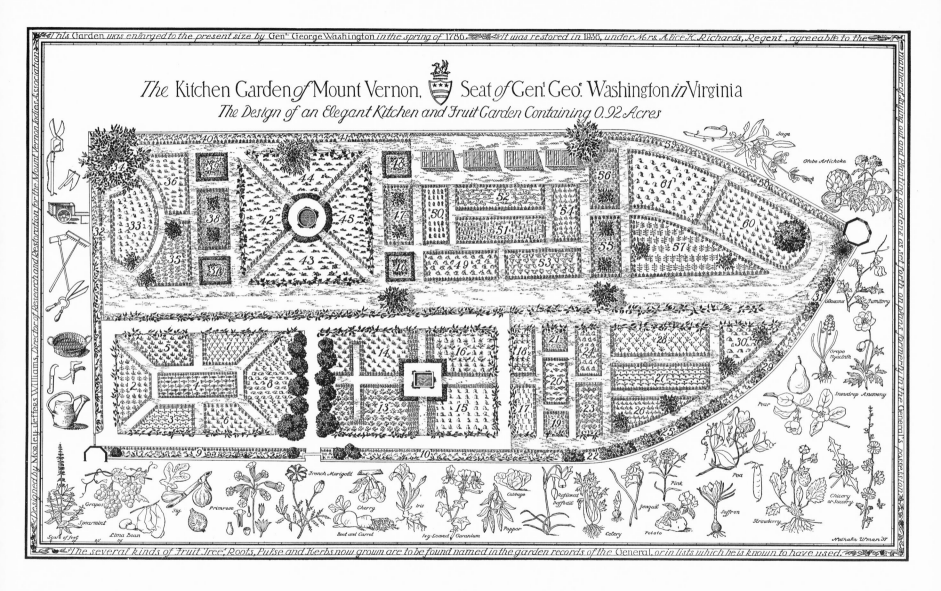

The Kitchen Garden of Mount Vernon, Seat of Genl. Geo. Washington in Virginia

The Design of an Elegant Kitchen and Fruit Garden Containing 0.92 Acres

Sage

Globe Artichoke

Glaucous

Fumitory

Grape Hyacinth

Snowdrop Anemony

Pear

Pea

Pink

Jonquil

Saffron

Strawberry

Chicory or Succory

French Marigold

Cherry

Iris

Cabbage

Reflexed Daffodil

Celery

Potato

Pepper

Ivy-Leaved Geranium

Beet and Carrot

Primrose

Fig

Grapes

Spearmint

Lima Bean

Scale of feet

Designed by Morley Jeffers Williams, Director of Research and Restoration for the Mount Vernon Ladies Association

Nathalia Ulman '38

Now the day has taken on its familiar summer aspect. The sun is flooding into the study, causing the temperature to rise rapidly on the thermometer Washington read and recorded faithfully each day. Heat pours in the open windows, and curtains hang limply on the sides. Only the central hall, its doors flung open at each end, brings a welcome draft through the house. The Washingtons and their guests often sat there to catch a breeze.

Left: The central hall

Below: The piazza

From a letter written by a Mount Vernon visitor in 1797: "This gallery is the place where the General and his family spend their afternoons with guests. . . ."

The Potomac seems to steam in the heat, and even the visitors who stop to rest on the piazza cannot seem to catch a refreshing breath of air. (In Washington's time thirty Windsor chairs were sometimes placed there for company.)

To Bryan Fairfax
July 4, 1774

I am very much engaged in raising one of the additions to my house, which I think (perhaps it is fancy) goes on better whilst I am present, than in my absense from the workmen.

Over the years, in two succeeding periods, the Mount Vernon mansion house was enlarged. Before bringing home his bride in 1759, with her two small children, Patsy and Jacky, Washington commissioned the first remodeling to be done. The modest four-room, story-and-a-half building where he had lived as a child was raised a full story and completely redecorated. By 1773 even these additions did not offer sufficient room for the family and the guests who were so numerous that Washington once laughingly referred to his house as "a well-resorted tavern!" He planned an addition at either end, on the north a Banquet Hall (more often referred to as "the New Room") and on the south a study on the first floor and, above, a master bedroom with adjoining dressing rooms for himself and Martha Washington. At the same time, the Colonnades were to be added to connect the two wing buildings, the kitchen and office, to the mansion on either side. Only the south addition was well under way before Washington left for Philadelphia in 1775, and the work was completed under Lund Washington's supervision during the war years. The piazza was paved with stone flagging and the pediment and cupola added after his retirement as Commander-in-Chief of the Army; they were finished by 1787. The outdoor work on each addition had to be done before cold weather arrived, so many summers rang with the noise of hammers and saws.

This morning the song of locusts has an end-of-summer sound; but the end is not yet here, and the cattle in the pasture move listlessly from one spot of shade to another as the sun moves, switching their tails and twitching their backs to chase away the flies.

The Banquet Hall mantle

Dining room ceiling. *To George Washington from Lund Washington, October, 1775: "The Stucco man is at work upon the dining room. God knows when he will get done."*

The Greenhouse is flooded with golden light, August sun patterning the paving-stone floor with the shadow of the arched window and the delicate mullions. After admiring an older "orangerie" at the Charles Carroll plantation, Mount Clare, in Maryland, Washington designed his own with great care; and its perfect proportions show the fine touch of his hand.

The reconstructed red brick building alongside the Upper Garden is empty now of most of its tubs of "exotic plants" except for a few jade plants which need protection even from mild summer winds. The potting benches are lined with baskets and empty clay pots. The Greenhouse, however, is by no means unoccupied! On a high shelf above the southeast door, a pair of doves have made their nest of twigs on top of a stack of pots. A window nearby is open at top and bottom, and the shy birds take turns flying in and out of the upper opening, one keeping the eggs warm while the other flies out for food.

Luckily, the gardener has a more modern supply of tools than those hanging on the wooden pegs below their little nest; for the doves obviously consider this shelf their own property and flutter nervously when an intruder approaches. In another week, the first chick will peck its way through its white shell and see for the first time this historic little corner.

Facing page: The Greenhouse

Above: Mount Vernon river landing

Right: View from the South Grove

August 23, 1786

With the Guinea grass Seed I had on hand, I began to make good the missing spaces of what was sowed in my small or Botanical Garden on the 13th of June last, but did not half finish it.

A black man working in the Botanical Garden wipes off the sweat that has trickled down his forehead below his stained hatband and continues his plaintive song. It rises and falls in a minor key as he pushes his wheelbarrow with a pace as lethargic as that of the river which somnolently laps the shore at the boat landing.

It is a good day for a ride on the riverboat that runs between Mount Vernon and Washington, D.C. ("The Federal City"). It may be an illusion, but the air doesn't seem as hot on the river; and even in the midday sun, Mount Vernon, nestling on its green hill like the dove on her nest, looks cooler than at close range.

From the boat it is obvious that Augustine Washington selected this spot for his house to catch every breeze that summer might send. It commands a view both upriver and down toward Chesapeake Bay. In a day when waterways were more important than highways, it was readily accessible to both the private and small commercial vessels that made their way to its landing to bring visitors, and load or deliver cargo.

September 18, 1768

My schooner sailed for Suffolk for a load of shingles.

The Potomac is not so blue or clear as in Washington's day or that earlier era when the Indians named it "River of Swans." Today's visitors would be ill-advised to go for a swim in her polluted waters as Washington did on hot afternoons like this one. Even Mount Vernon's small fishing fleet would have trouble today finding enough shad or herring to keep their seines filled. The riverboat passes the cove where the old Fish House once stood. When the tide was right, and word went out across the plantation that fish were running, it came alive with activity.

The white fish ran plentifully at my Sein landing having catchd abt. 300 in one Hawl.

If the boats came in at night, as they often did, the flickering orange light of bonfires and flambeaux lit their way to shore, the firelight playing on black faces and white. Boats and wagons from neighboring farms arrived at the Fish House with eager buyers. Washington's own people knew that part of the catch was theirs for the asking; and the anticipation of a fresh fish dinner brought men and children scurrying to the landing while women got the cooking fires blazing in the Quarters. Little youngsters too small to

The Storehouse on the North Lane
January 3, 1760: "Hauled the Seine and got some fish."

join the happy caravan to the river were kept occupied by setting the trestle tables with their wooden plates and forks or spoons.

Empty barrels and a good supply of salt were quickly drawn from the Storehouse and loaded into the cart which rattled off down the lane at as rapid a pace as the mule could be threatened into making. As it reached the landing, the seines were being hauled in, many hands pulling together on the heavy nets. Then the fish not immediately claimed for supper tables were cleaned, salted down in their barrels, and the tops nailed in place; while carts carried away the offal to be used as fertilizer on Mount Vernon fields. . . .

Now the riverboat is passing Gunston Cove, not putting into it as Washington sometimes did, tying his boat at the landing of Gunston Hall, home of his neighbor, Colonel George Mason.

The two masters of Mount Vernon and Gunston Hall had much to talk about besides the affairs of Pohick Church, where both were vestrymen, and their occasional fox hunts together. On the politics of the Commonwealth of Virginia, the colonies, and later the new United States, they shared the same goals. When Mason penned the Virginia Declaration of Rights in 1776, which later formed the basis of the Federal

The Quarters

The Salt House

Bill of Rights, he had Washington's full support. The two men fell out, however, over the adoption of the U.S. Constitution, which Mason opposed because he felt that human rights were inadequately guaranteed. Washington believed the door was open for their adoption later (as indeed soon happened), and that the union of the new states was so fragile it would fall apart without the Constitution's immediate adoption.

Mason stood firm on another point with which Washington agreed—the moral and practical necessity of freeing the slaves.

To his nephew, Lawrence Lewis
August 4, 1797

Your letter of the 24th ulto has been received, and I am sorry to hear of the loss of your servant; but it is my opinion that these elopements will by MUCH MORE, before they are LESS frequent; and . . . I wish from my soul that the Legislature of this State could see the policy of a gradual Abolition of Slavery. It would prevent much future mischief.

The thrum of the old riverboat's motors vibrate the deck as she turns and makes her way back—past Dogue Creek and on to Ferry Point across from Marshall Hall where Captain John Posey once owned the ferry slip which Washington purchased.

From across the water, the cupola of Mount Vernon appears first above the

Washington's writing table in the library

Down the stairs
to the model of the
Bastille in the central hall

trees, its weathervane moving little in the still August air—a heart-lifting sight for Mount Vernon's owner as he rounded a bend of the river on many journeys. For a man who never really wanted to leave home, it was the first visible sign that he was almost there—back to the land he loved and the people who meant most to him.

The boat pulls into the dock, and the slight breeze she carried with her stays willfully on the river.

It is mid-afternoon. It is hot. It is summer at Mount Vernon.

August 4, 1768

But little rain with great appearance of a settled Rain afternoon tho not enough to make the House eves Run.

The rain started in the night—a refreshing sound on the shingled roof, so deceptively gentle a patter that it didn't immediately signal sleepers to check the windows. By morning the sills are wet, a few puddles are on the floor, and there is much scurrying for towels to mop up.

Rain blows up suddenly along the river. Mount Vernon is such a large house—and with no passageway through from the Washingtons' bedroom to those on the other side in the eighteenth century—what a flurry a shower must have caused. The house servants would be running up and down the stairs, then around to the other side and up again, and up still another flight to get the windows down in the garret rooms.

The rain has brought the temperature down, and only a little wind is blowing, so it is pleasant to walk in it down the Serpentine Paths. The parched grass and trees along the Bowling Green are drinking up the welcome moisture after days of searing heat. Already they look greener.

A garret room
where visiting staff members
stayed

Below and facing page:
The Kitchen Garden

To Tobias Lear
July 30, 1792

The day & night we reached home, there fell a most delightful & refreshing rain, and the weather since has been as seasonable as the most sanguine farmer could wish, and if continued to us may make our Indian Corn crop midling—great it is hardly possible to be —so much was it in arrears when the rains set in.

The wind picks up, and now the drops are coming down harder, making little rivulets of the gutters down the South Lane. The Kitchen Garden, where leaves on some of the vegetables had begun to turn yellow in spite of the gardener's careful watering, has a fresher look already. In the moist air, the tomato plants have a pungent, musky odor, and the wet herbs—the thyme, the tarragon, sweet marjoram and basil— give off a potpourri of scents.

As you round the courtyard, the wind blows gustily under the

honeysuckle-covered Colonnades and threatens to turn umbrellas inside out. The rain has collected on the painted wooden benches, and the water makes a mirror for the cupola's reflection. If the Washingtons were in residence, this would be a good day for a game of cards in the parlor, or for Martha Washington to bring out her quilting or her knitting needles. It is a day for enjoying the pleasant solitude with one's own family.

To Tobias Lear
July 31, 1797

Unless some one pops in, unexpectedly—Mrs. Washington & myself will do what I believe has not been done within the last twenty Years by us,—that is to set down to dinner by ourselves.

Beyond the North Grove, the pasture sloping down to the riverbank looks lush and green, giving a promise of richer milk from the cows, as Martha Washington remembered when she wrote from Philadelphia to Fanny at Mount Vernon. Watching the rain fall on dusty city streets, her thoughts turned wistfully back to the country:

August 4, 1793

This fine wet summer I should think there must be a great quantity of Butter made— which might be sold to bye such necessaries as one wanted about the House— as it will be needless to put up a large quantity for winter.

The cupola reflected in a rain pool

The parlor

At the reconstructed Grist Mill, rain is splashing into the usually quiet creek, which widens here before it disappears under the bridge. The water in the mill race and in Dogue Run, which had been low and muddy all week, is rising rapidly—a sight that would have delighted Washington's eyes. To Washington's distress, when the water level was down, production at the mill slowed to a mere trickle. One such day in 1760 he was caught at the mill by a thunder shower, and decided to see exactly how long it took for one bushel of corn to be ground, from the time the miller poured it into the hopper on the first floor and engaged the gears of the water wheel until it returned as corn meal to the ground floor container.

[Experimented] on what time the mill requir'd to grind a bushel of corn, and to my Surprize found she was within 5 minutes of an hour about this. Old Anthony attributed to the low head of water, but whether it was so or not I can't say—her works [being] all decayed and out of Order which I rather take to be the cause.

After consistently disappointing results from the mill in spite of frequent repairs, he rebuilt it in 1770; and during his second term as President, had the mill race reconstructed.

I rid to my Mill with [John] Ball and agreed with him to build her.

The Colonnade

The old tree at the door of the mill is the same one that spread its shade there in Washington's day. Tradition has it that once it was struck by lightning, but that dripping sap from the wounded tree put out the beginnings of a fire at her roots— a nice story, whether true or apochryphal.

The rain drips from the tree's branches in a musical rhythm. The sky begins to lighten even though it is near the hour of sunset. Tomorrow may be clear. . . .

1767

. . .Clear, Warm and pleasant. According to Colo. West, ye greatest part of the next Moon should be as this one i.e. the same kind of weather that happens upon Thurs. before the change will continue through ye course of the next Moon, at least the first and second quarter of it. Quere—is not this an old woman's story?

Beyond the paddock, the sun sets behind low clouds, blue and thin and ruffled like white caps on the river blown by the wind. In the east, the full moon appears at almost the same moment. It comes up against a buttermilk sky, huge and luminous, neither silver nor gold but seemingly incandescent. With unbelieveable speed, it rises across the Potomac.

One moment it is swinging like a giant globe through the locusts in the North Grove, just above the Colonnade. In the next—in the time it takes to walk around the circle from the office to the Storehouse on the other side—it has almost cleared the treetops.

One of the guards making his evening rounds calls softly across the green, "Look quick—up by the gate houses! The deer are grazing!" You turn quickly, and in the half-moonlight, half-sunset glow, you can just make out the graceful leap of a fawn back by the West Gate, and see the forms of the dignified elders of the flock that have ventured out from the trees into the meadow. There is a flash of snow white that is gone almost as quickly as it came—and you realize you have caught a glimpse of the rare white deer that are seen occasionally at Mount Vernon. Can they be descended from the fawns Washington once imported for his "deer park," hoping their grazing would keep the grass down?

To Colonel William Fairfax, 1785

Mr. Ogle of Maryland has been so obliging as to present me six fawns from his park of English deer at Bellair. With these, and tolerable care, I should soon have a full stock for my small paddock.

Now it is "the dawn of Candlelight," and as though the faithful Bishop or one of the house servants were moving with his taper from room to room,

Night deepens as the moon rises over the plantation.

soft lights wink on in the windows, one by one. As the sky turns deeper blue, the moon is almost golden as are the running lights of a tug and barge headed upstream on the river below.

Since 1801, the bells of river boats have saluted Mount Vernon as they passed. Even British Admiral Sir George Cockburn, sailing down the Potomac after raiding Alexandria, tolled his ship's bell in respect as he passed; and the gesture became a tradition. In 1853, with a full moon bathing the old white mansion, a steamboat's bell awakened one passenger in time to see the sad disrepair into which it had fallen—its roof sagging, one pillar missing, the lawn overgrown. Mrs. Robert Cunningham of South Carolina wrote of the scene to her semi-invalid daughter, Ann Pamela; and the young woman launched an incredibly ambitious plan for the women of the country to buy the first President's home and keep it for the nation. The moon tonight reveals the success of the Mount Vernon Ladies' Association.

A pigeon flies to the top of the pediment over the ox-eye window above the courtyard. Cooing sleepily, it settles down, a feathered silhouette outlined against the bright moon. Above it, the copper dove of peace, carrying its olive branch, swings gently on the weathervane's axis. The birds of two centuries keep watch in the quiet summer night.

September 6, 1768

My ox cart finished drawing in the wheat at Doeg Run, but during this time it was [also] employed in getting home the Cyder from all the Plantations.

Fall

Frost silvered the grass this morning. A fragrance of wood smoke is in the air as children in bright sweaters shuffle through the dry leaves on the Bowling Green and along the Serpentine Walks. The smoke is drifting up the South Lane on an autumn breeze from Hell Hole— the wooded land by the river which earned its name, deservedly, two hundred years ago when it was marshland. The summer's tangle of underbrush is being cleared and burned; and nearby, the huge woodpiles for Mount Vernon fireplaces are growing, the burr of the saw and ring of the ax punctuating the morning stillness.

There are other unmistakable signs that fall is here. A dogwood tree on the east lawn is brilliant orange-red; and the locust trees, which Washington prized for their spring bloom, have turned to an equally dramatic yellow this early October. The pods of the magnolia are covered with bright scarlet seeds which the usually shy pilated woodpeckers consider to be a feast set out especially for them. Beyond the kitchen (when Martha Washington was in charge,

The courtyard and Bowling Green from the cupola

it would have been fragrant with bubbling apple butter and currant jelly in this season), two chestnut trees flaunt their handsome orange brown leaves.

From Martha Washington

Tom brings you 37 lb. of butter which is all that could be put into pots. We intended to come to see you this week but Jack told us you would come some day but did not say what day. . . . There is a cask of apples here for you. Mr. Wa'n would have sent them, but he had no barrell that the Mallojes could be put in or should send them boath to you.

Grapes in the Kitchen Garden are ripening. Carrot tops are rich and feathery, and fall lettuce and onion plants have been set out. The eggplant are lushly purple on their vines, although the leaves are beginning to turn brown. A cardinal is gossiping from the top of the brick wall.

In the Upper Garden, the paths are freshly raked, although this is a constant chore which every wind through the tulip poplars and the ash trees makes futile. Hibiscus are blooming in the Greenhouse which is still only sparsely occupied by plants. Within a few weeks, at the first sign of frost, it will be filled with the lemon trees and cactus and sago palms. In the loft, flowers and herbs have been hung up to dry for use this winter, and seeds have been spread in flats for next year's planting.

The Kitchen Garden and the Necessary House (at far end of fence)

A farm road that bends and becomes the North Lane

Left:
The ox-eye window
in the Greenhouse attic

Facing page, above:
The Fairfax County Hunt
whose beagle hounds are
believed to be descended
from Washington's pack

Facing page, below:
Signature of Martha
Washington's granddaughter
Eliza Custis, aged 10, in the
yellow bedroom window

Blue haze hangs over the Potomac, and the green hills beyond are splashed with pastel yellow and orange foliage. In the eighteenth century, this was a favorite time for traveling by boat, and the Washington family could expect visitors at any hour.

October 2, 1785

After we were in Bed (about eleven Oclock in the Evening) Mr. Houdon, sent from Paris by Dr. Franklin and Mr. Jefferson to take my Bust, in behalf of the state of Virginia, with three young assistants . . . arrived here by Water from [Alexandria].

In September, 1793, Washington traveled upstream to "the Federal City" for an important occasion—the laying of the cornerstone of the Capitol of the United States.

The Washingtons could count on spending some time at home nearly every fall from 1789 to 1797, after Congress adjourned for its annual recess. Martha knew this meant family visits—happy reunions with her other Custis grandchildren (her namesake, Martha Parke, and lively Eliza, the older sisters of Nelly and Washie) and Martha's sisters and brothers and their families. State visitors, too, frequently arrived at the President's home on the Potomac during these vacations, and Martha anticipated this probability with what seems like small enthusiasm.

From Martha Washington
to Fanny Bassett Washington
Philadelphia, July 1, 1792

I wish my dear Fanny that you would make Frank clanse the House from the garret to the sellers—have all the Beds aird and mended and the Bed Clothes of every kind made very clean. The Bedsteads also wett scalded—and the low bedsteads put up to be ready to carry out of one room into another as you know they are often wanted—I have not a doubt but we shall have company all the time we are at home.

From the piazza, the sun glints like silver on the river which mirrors the blue October sky. Along the North Lane, shadows are etched on the white wall of the Spinning House, the partially bare branches of the locusts outlined through the willows' lace. Behind the brick wall, near the Ice House, toadstools have popped up like elves' umbrellas.

Squirrels are growing bolder each day —darting up to open doors in the Quarters, the bootmaker's shop, even the mansion house, and peering in like a prospective tenant looking for his winter's residence. They are getting fatter, furrier, and more curious, acorns bulging their cheeks as they search busily for a safe hiding place.

The cawing of crows seems more insistent, one flock wheeling and circling over the garden, then taking off across the meadow toward the river.

Above:
Spinning House quarters

Left:
Spinning House

Facing page:
Shoemaker's Shop

Still at home all day Plotting and measuring the Surveys which Captn. Crawford made for the Officers and Soldiers.

Washington used his experience as a surveyor that autumn to check the survey notes on boundaries of the lands given by the British to him and his fellow soldiers who had fought against the French and their Indian allies. Even such worthy business must have left him restless when October air blew invitingly through the study windows. But the House of Burgesses would soon be meeting, and he must be ready to head for Williamsburg. It is hard weather to stay indoors, with all of the Mount Vernon countryside to ride before winter puts her lock on the land. The sun is warm on your back as you strike out across the fields.

The leaves of wild blackberry bushes, growing along the split rail fence, which have already yielded their clusters of small sweet-sour berries, are beginning to turn red. Look closer, and you see a few strawberry plants growing along fence posts. How did they get here? Are they wild ones, or the remnants of a cultivated patch? Or did a bird drop the seeds here inadvertently on a flight from the Kitchen Garden?

A few late dandelions dot the brown meadow with white silk pincushions of seed; and an errant Monarch

Left: Pyracantha bush

Quince

A Mount Vernon resident

French honeysuckle

Dwarf zinnias

butterfly drifts on the October breeze in the same dance step as the gently falling yellow leaves.

A quince bush guards its ripe golden fruit between long thorns, but some enterprising jam-maker is sure to find a way to pick it before long. The wind in the trees is not yet the clatter of late fall, but a rustle that is noisier, higher pitched than in summer. Two dry old elm branches talk, as it blows, like the clack of a pair of ill-fitting dentures.

Among the gnarled roots of other trees, a delicate member of the mushroom family has overnight put out exquisite beige petals among the brown leaves. Somewhere a dog yips excitedly as if he scented a rabbit.

It is almost noon, and time to turn back and head up the hill again. A pyracantha bush studded with orange berries, framing a glimpse of the mansion house above, catches you in a spell half Indian Summer, half Allhallows Eve. This is the sort of path—uncut and full of brambles— that a boy would be sure to find on a fall day as he comes home with scuffed shoes and dusty trousers. Somehow, in the noonday sun, ahead of you seems to run Jacky Custis—or is it his son, little Washie, a generation later, who climbs up the hill just out of reach and calls loudly to his grandmother, Martha Washington, like any hungry boy, "What's for dinner?"

Morning clear. Wind at No. Wt. and Mer. at 36. From 10 o'clock until 2 very like for Snow, it then cleared and became mild and pleasant.

Winter

A column of smoke rises from the tall chimney of the Quarters, pale against a grayer sky, and the wind sends it curling down through the magnolia trees. Their dark waxy leaves are a welcome contrast to the stark bare branches of the locusts and elms, the pecans and maples. The slate-colored river is angry-looking; and in the clear cold air, the sound of waves churning against the shore below carries across the brown meadow. A small oyster boat heads downriver to the Bay.

A gust of wind hurtles down the North Lane, pushing an armload of dry brown leaves before it; and some of them catch in the bars of the gates and pile up behind them. During the night, the lazy, hazy spell of a long Indian Summer was broken abruptly by a storm, and winter has definitely arrived at Mount Vernon.

Fortunately, the warm days of late November gave the winter rye grass planted on the courtyard and Bowling Green time to get a good start, and its surprising luxuriant green softens the bleakness of the winter scene.

The barometer in the central hall of the mansion is still falling at 9 o'clock, and clouds on the horizon seem to threaten snow by evening. In December, when everyone hopes for a "white Christmas," this seems more like a promise.

Everything has slowed to a winter's pace at Mount Vernon. All the tropical plants have been moved into the Greenhouse, which holds them like a little island of summer; and the mulched garden outside looks "bedded down" for the season. There was ice this morning on the dipping well, and a single icicle on the corner of the office roof, under the eaves. Few visitors stroll along the empty walks; and down the South Lane, the only sign of life is the scarlet flash of a cardinal.

In the eighteenth century, too, the rhythm of life at Mount Vernon changed in December but perhaps not as drastically as now. Activity varied as the weather did, but a working plantation required constant care at every time of year.

December 22, 1786

Rid to the Neck, Muddy hole, Dogue run and Ferry Plantations. Getting wheat into the Barn at the first; threshing it at the 2d; about finished gathering Corn at the 3d; and cutting down Corn stalks for the Farm pen at the last.

When the harvest was in, the grain in the Storehouse for next year's

Mr. Butler's quarters behind the Storehouse

The Quarters behind the Greenhouse

The Storehouse

To Howell Lewis, August 11, 1793: "The Clover Seed which went from hence in July, in a cask the size of a flax barrel . . . Mr. Lear says he put in the Store himself—consequently, if it is not there now, Butler must be made answerable for it."

planting, little field work could be done; and men were free to work on cutting roads, clearing fields for pastures, running fences. At all seasons, the livestock had to be cared for, especially when snow covered the feed lots. The ice—or lack of it—on the river also rearranged plans sometimes.

December 15, 1786

The River in the Ferry way became entirely free of Ice this morning, and my Boats and hands which had been froze up on the Maryland side since Saturday last returned.

When the Potomac froze solid, its hard surface provided a vantage point from which Washington could use his tripod and theodolite to check the property's boundaries as he had done on Lord Fairfax's land when he was only sixteen.

January 21, 1768

Surveyed the water course of my Mount Vernon tract of land, taking advantage of the Ice.

A squirrel patters distractedly along the Serpentine Path, looking from right to left. Has he forgotten where he buried all those nuts last fall? With sudden determination he bounds toward the gate in the Kitchen Garden wall. The garden itself lies dormant, all its harvest preserved for the winter table.

People are converging on the mansion house today from all directions in a December scene familiar to Virginians and their British antecedents for generations—Christmas greens are being brought in to "deck the halls" for the holidays. The woods by the West Gate and behind the pastures have been searched for the choicest boughs of pine and spruce and cedar, and the pruning of holly and boxwood has been timed to provide fresh green cuttings. Just as a gardener, huddled into a plaid wool lumber jacket, arrives with a wheelbarrow of fragrant evergreen branches, a shop worker comes around the courtyard carrying a tall ladder for hanging the boughs above doors in the Banquet Hall and the central hall. The cook brings over a large basket of fresh fruit from the kitchen for the dining table centerpiece; and ladies adept at making decorations hurry in out of the wind, armed with their shears, wire, and wooden picks for keeping the fruit in place on their decorations. Clearly, the happy holiday season is on its way at Mount Vernon.

December 20, 1785

Brought some Carts and Cutters from my Plantations to assist in laying in a Stock of Firewood for Christmas.

The Washingtons and their neighbors celebrated the holidays simply but merrily. Plantation workers and

The North Lane gates

To Thomas Law, December 25, 1797: "We . . . all unite in offering you, & yours, the compliments of the Season."

craftsmen had several days off from their chores, and bonfires blazed at night by the Quarters. Kitchen fires snapped and crackled, while the aroma of fruit and mince pies, roasting capons stuffed with oyster dressing, and hams and fresh bread baking drifted out to warm the passersby with promises of a feast to come.

In their red waistcoats and dark blue or pink hunting coats, men from nearby plantations rode up to join in pursuit of the wily fox—which then, as now, seems to have involved far more pursuing than catching! To arm the riders with a Christmas stirrup cup or to cheer them at the hunt's end, the Master of Mount Vernon ladled out his usual holiday eggnog from a Lowestoft bowl. Its ingredients are awe-inspiring: one quart milk, one quart cream, one dozen eggs, one dozen tablespoons of sugar, one pint brandy, one-half pint rye whiskey, one-fourth pint Jamaica or New England rum, and one-fourth pint sherry. The mixture was set in a cool place for several days, during which the General—if he followed the recipe's instructions—"tasted frequently" to be sure it was aging properly.

The most memorable eighteenth-century Christmas Eve at Mount Vernon took place in 1782. At Annapolis two days before, he had formally resigned his commission as Commander-in-Chief of the Army, "commending the interests of our dear country to the protection of Almighty God; and those who have the superintendence of them to His holy keeping." Early the next morning he rode south for home, accompanied by his aides, Colonels David Humphreys, William Smith, and Benjamin Walker.

They approached the Mount Vernon gates at dusk, the lights of Christmas bonfires adding to the festive welcome of "his people," Martha Washington, and his two little grandchildren, Nelly and Washie, bubbling with the excitement of any youngsters on Christmas Eve. After eight years Mount Vernon's master was in residence again; and "home for Christmas" was a reality deep with meaning, deeper perhaps with children living in the house again. (On an earlier Christmas in 1759, their father Jack, his little sister Patsy, and Martha all had the chicken pox!)

Unless the weather made roads impassable, six horses were harnessed to the coach on Christmas morning, and it was brought around to the courtyard door to take the family the nine miles over winter-rutted roads to the special worship service that celebrated the birth of the Infant Christ.

December 25, 1771

Went to Pohick Church with Mrs. Washington and returned to dinner.

Above: The parlor

Facing page:
Christmas dessert course
in the dining room

The cook's art took over now as steaming trays of food were carried by quick-stepping servants from the kitchen, under the Colonnade, and through the mansion house door to the dining room. Here all the members of the family and guests of the house were gathered around the table for "the blessed feast of Christmas."

Today that table is being set for an after-dessert course. Martha Washington's blue and white Canton china has been replaced by plates from an identical set which she and the President presented to their close friend, Mrs. Samuel Powel, of Philadelphia just before they left that city to retire to Mount Vernon. Dishes of black walnuts, glazed cherries, almonds and golden raisins, gaily topped with holly, are ready to be passed; and the Washington decanters hold white and red wines. In the center is a fruit pyramid, topped by a pineapple, the colonial symbol of hospitality; and at each place is a round blue water bowl, used by guests for rinsing their wine glasses between the many courses of a holiday meal.

To Colonel David Humphreys
December 26, 1786

Altho I lament the effect, I am pleased at the cause which has deprived us of the pleasure of your aid in the attack of Christmas pies: we had one yesterday on which all the company, tho pretty numerous, were hardly able to make an impression.

As the last bit of boxwood is arranged in the black lacquer monteith in the hall, the last spruce bough is hung above the door to the piazza, the last spray of holly placed on the nut dish, one of the ladies in the dining room glances through the frosted window to the courtyard.

"It's snowing!" she cries in delight, and everyone rushes over to see. Sure enough, the snow is falling as gently as goose down escaping from a pillow. It is clinging to the trees and putting furry caps on the sundial and fence posts. Boots, coats, and scarves are donned, and the group makes its way out into the winter dusk. A hush lies over Mount Vernon. Footsteps are muffled in the snow; yellow light glows through a few windows; and you can almost hear the jingle of sleigh bells coming down the lane. . . .

If Washington stopped in at Purdie and Dixon's printing office in Williamsburg while the House of Burgesses was meeting in the fall of 1770, he may have bought a copy of *The Virginia Almanack for the Year of our Lord God 1771.* If so, he may have read this Christmas note following their calendar for December:
"We wish you health, and good fires; victuals, drink, and good stomachs; innocent diversion, and good company; honest trading, and good success; loving courtship, and good wives; and lastly, a merry CHRISTMAS and a happy NEW YEAR."

The music room

To Clement Biddle, December 21, 1789:
"Mrs. Washington will be much obliged to you to get from Mr. Reinagle who taught Miss [Nelly] Custis music last summer, such music as he may think proper for her to progress through the winter."

December 29, 1786

The hollidays being over, and the People all at work, I rid to the Ferry, Dogue run, and Muddy hole Plantations.

The snow melts, and new snow falls. Fires burn down, and logs must be carried in again. A bitter wind blows across the river one day, and the next is soft as a kitten's paw; mornings are blue, but even the sun looks cold and distant. For the Washington family, it was the season for bedwarmers, music lessons, or tea in the parlor by a cozy fire. Nothing has changed too much today.

When snow is on the ground, the wild animals are more often seen as they search for food, and the guard reports he saw the deer last night on the north lawn.

January 1, 1768

Fox hunting in my own Neck with Mr. Robert Alexander and Mr. Colville. Catched nothing.

January 29, 1769

At home all day, opening the Avenue to the House . . . and for bringing the Road along.

Repairs are made while the weather is too cold for outside work. Letters must be written, and life beyond Mount Vernon boundaries affects the schedule of events as they did two centuries ago—visits by foreign dignitaries and Presidential parties come and go. Echoes of war are heard faintly here, more faintly than when British warships made their way up the Potomac.

To Lund Washington
January 31, 1776

The Bacon when it is sufficiently smoked, I think to have put up in casks with ashes and if necessary (because of fighting) move it, together with some Pork which I have already put up in barrels. . . .

Deliveries are held up, by bad weather or bad service. Newspapers are sometimes late.

To Clement Biddle, Philadelphia
February 1, 1785

I do not know how to account for it, but so the fact is, that altho I am a Subscriber to Messrs. Dunlap and Claypoole's Packet and Daily Advertiser, I do not get one paper in five of them. . . . let me know the cause of my disappointments. . . .

The winter social season brings friends together in Fairfax County homes and at Gadsby's Tavern in Alexandria for its traditional Birthnight Ball on February 22, (the Washingtons attended the first of these gala celebrations in 1784). It was somewhat different than one to which Washington took his bride during her first winter at Mount Vernon.

The study. *June 16, 1786: "Began about 10 O'clock to put up the Book presses in my study."*

Left: The bedroom where Lafayette stayed
on visits to Mount Vernon

Below, left: Believed to be the bedroom
of George Washington Parke Custis (Washie)

Below, right: Nelly Custis's bedroom

February 15, 1760

*Went to a Ball at Alexandria, where
Musick and Dancing were the chief
Entertainment. However in a convenient
Room detachd for the purpose abounded great
plenty of Bread and Butter, some Biscuits
with Tea, and Coffee which the Drinkers of
could not distinguish from Hot water
sweetened. Be it remembered that pocket
handkerchiefs servd the purposes of Table
Cloths and Napkins and that no Apologies
were made for either. . . . I shall therefore
distinguish this Ball by the Stile and title of
the Bread and Butter Ball.*

Winter is a sometime thing here, now
crisp and cold and invigorating, now
damp and miserable with snow falling,
melting, falling again to hang on both
evergreen and bare branches in
breathtaking beauty.

March 19, 1768

*. . . abt 8 oclock began Snowing which it did
constantly the whole day from the No. Et.
and was one of the most disagreeable days of
the whole winter.*

Suddenly one morning, the first green
finger of a crocus thrusts out through
the snow in the Upper Garden; and
the birds at sunrise in the bare crape
myrtle trees seem to be bursting with
good news. A robin is seen on the
brick wall behind the bell along the
South Lane; and the ewes, penned in
the paddock because it is almost

The South Lane. At left, the kitchen; at right, the Storehouse and Mr. Butler's quarters;
beyond, the Smokehouse, Wash House, and Coach House

The kitchen with roast turkey garnished with flowers in the eighteenth-century manner

The cupola

lambing time, shake their thick wool coats and move awkwardly out to warm themselves in a patch of sun.

February 10, 1786

This day was remarkable fine and promotive of vegeatation. The buds of the lylack much swelled and seemed ready to unfold.

Buds appear on the dogwood, and the cows are let out into pastures that are turning green with winter rye watered by melting snows.

In the Upper Garden, the gardener is raking the mulch from around the daffodil and tulip bulbs, and his young helper is setting out spring onions in the Kitchen Garden. Tomorrow he will plant early peas and start pepper and tomato plants in the cold frames.

Somewhere a farmer steps out of his front door, beginning his day with sunrise, as Washington did. He smells the fresh breeze blowing off the Potomac across winter-dormant fields, and says, "It's almost time for plowing." And another man, or it may be the same one, will find himself—a few miles upriver—struggling with a decision that will embark him on a wide ocean in which perhaps there may be no safe harbor. But he, too, will turn, no matter how reluctantly, to feel the wind on his face as he sails out. . . .

And any day, any bright blue day, it will be spring again at Mount Vernon.

She with the silent pen

8 Clear, brisk southerly wind
Mer 65 — Mr Stuart & two other
Daughters came to dinner as
did Mr Lear — Mr La Tombe went a—

9 Wind brisk from the No. W.
& turning cold — Mer 64.
Mr Lear & Mr Peter went a—

10 The wind continuing at No W
it grew colder — Mer at 58 —

11 Wind at No W. & fresh after
the morning Mer at 56 — Mr
Stuart & Daughters & Mr Pe—
ter went after break fast

12 Cold & frosty morning Mer 54
Mr & G. W. La Fayette & Mr Frestel
left this for Geo Town to take
the Stage for New York to em
bark for France — I accompa
nied them to the Fed City

13 I returned home to dinner
Capt Spence dined here & went
away afterwards — Mer at
wind Southerly

14 Great appearances of
Rain — but none fell. Wind
Southerly — Mer 54 — Mr Mc
Donald & Mr Rich Brit Cons
came to dinner —

Christopher set out for de
baner

15 Clear & pleasant calm in the
morning — wind at No W. after
Mer at 58 — Mr Potts & Mr Keith
dined here & returned

16 Clear & moderate with but little
wind — Mer 55 — Mr Macdonald
& Mr Rich went away after break
fast Mr Nicholas — & Mr & Mrs Nichols
& wife & Doct Stuart came to din
Mr Jenifer returned after it —

17 Clear and pleasant — Doct
Stuart went away after break
fast — Mr Law & Cap Turner
came in the after. Mer 59

18 Clear & pleasant — wind West
Mer 61 — Mr Law & Cap Turner
went away after breakfast &
Mr Geo. Calvert came to din

19 calm & very pleasant — M 58

20 Cloudy morning with the wind
at No E. — Abt noon it began to
Rain & cont'd to do so more or less
all day — Mer at 56 —

21 Wind still at No E. & misting all
day Mer at 56 — Mr Calvert
went away after breakfast

22 Clear and dry — wind at No W. M 57
Mr Potts & wife & Mr Smith & wife
& Mr Lear dined here —

23 Very clear & pleasant — M. 56
went there the family to din
er & M Mr Potts in Alexandria